THE BEST OF ANGUS OG

EWEN BAIN

INTRODUCTION AND COMMENTARY BY SHEILA BAIN

MAINSTREAM
PUBLISHING

First published in Great Britain 1990 by
MAINSTREAM PUBLISHING COMPANY (EDINBURGH) LTD
7 Albany Street
Edinburgh EH1 3UG

British Library Cataloguing in Publication Data
Bain, Ewen
   The best of angus og.
   1. Scottish humorous cartoons
   I. Title
   741.59411

   ISBN 1-85158-377-7

Typeset in Univers
Printed in Great Britain by Scotprint Ltd, Musselburgh

CONTENTS

TO EWEN AND ALL FRIENDS
WHO, BY THEIR ENCOURAGEMENT,
MADE THE PUBLICATION OF
THIS BOOK POSSIBLE.

INTRODUCTION

It was midsummer when Ewen Campbell Bain was born in Maryhill, Glasgow, on 23 June 1925, the youngest of three children born to John and Flora Bain from the Isle of Skye. His father from Waternish and his mother from Staffin had moved to Glasgow after their marriage in 1912. Surrounded by the tenements and streets of Maryhill they never forgot the lovely island they had left, and their city home became a place of Highland hospitality where Ewen's first words would undoubtedly have been in Gaelic.

Ewen had very happy memories of his childhood in Glasgow where a favourite treat was a walk with his father to see the ships lined along the busy docks on Clydeside — sadly empty today! Margaret, his sister, does not remember Ewen drawing much at home though he was good at art in school. She does remember him clowning and carrying-on with herself and his brother, James. When this got out of hand, the two older children would get a row from their parents, but rarely Ewen. He told me that he escaped trouble by making them laugh: this I can believe as he used the same tactics with me!

He had even happier memories of idyllic summer holidays. Each year at the beginning of July there was great excitement when the hamper was brought out for packing — the signal for the early-morning departure on the train to Mallaig where MacBrayne's steamer was waiting to speed them over the sea to Skye. Ewen's mother stayed with the children during July and August and there was more excitement when their father arrived in Staffin for his annual holiday. This was much more than a family holiday — it was 'coming home' and the welcome, of course, would be in Gaelic.

Ewen loved Skye and was very keen that I should share its magic with him. My choice of view to express that magic would be of rounding the bend of the road at the monument in Staffin to behold the superb Quiraing against a lilac, evening sky with Brogaig and Stenscholl spread below it. Following that would be the welcome awaiting us at Riverside.

The carefree summers of Ewen's boyhood ended with the advent of the Second World War. His brother was already in the Merchant Navy when Ewen left Woodside Senior Secondary School to enrol in the Glasgow School of Art. Before he was called up, during his first year, to join the Royal Navy he had to take his share of the firewatching rota in the famous Mackintosh building. 'A skylark', he called it, never being one to take life too seriously.

Ewen trained as a coder and spent most of the war sailing between Gibraltar and West Africa on convoy-escort duty. He had funny stories about his wartime experiences. It would happen to Ewen, of course, that his office was in the bowels of the ship next to the ammunition store.

When he was demobbed he returned to Glasgow School of Art where he was one of the many ex-servicemen and women who had priority of entry. School-leavers were seriously outnumbered — seriously, that is, for the boys — but delightful for the girls. It was there that we met as students and we married in Glasgow in 1950. I can remember only one cartoon at that time, which was published in *Ygorra*, the students' charities magazine.

Ewen trained as a teacher in Jordanhill College of Education and taught in a number of schools in Glasgow until he left in 1969 for a full-time career as a cartoonist. He started drawing single cartoons to supplement our income when I resigned from teaching after our daughter, Rhona, was born in 1955. To guard against disappointment from early rejections, he always made sure that several batches of cartoons were in the post. It was a great thrill when some were accepted and the welcome cheques arrived.

His talent spotted, he was advised to attempt a strip cartoon and from this encouragement Angus Og (young Angus) was created, his first adventure appearing in the Glasgow *Bulletin* in 1960. Shortly after that the *Bulletin* ceased publication and 'Angus Og' joined the *Daily Record* and later the *Sunday Mail.*

It was midwinter when Ewen died suddenly and unexpectedly on 18 December 1989, from pneumonia which developed swiftly during a bad attack of 'flu. This was a dark day for me and, though I greatly miss his cheerful, kindly presence, the brightness of his humour lives on in the adventures of Angus Og.

Sheila Bain
September 1990

1960

A TEEN-AGE TANGLE O' THE ISLES

or

THE ENCHANTED CHANTER

Angus, depressed and lonely since Mairileen went away to work in the distillery, consoles himself by going to the moor to play his chanter. Hearing a cry for help, Angus finds a strange, little man stuck in a bog. He is one of the 'wee folk', who rewards Angus for rescuing him by putting a magic spell on his chanter.

Angus enthralls all who hear him play the enchanted chanter.

He becomes a local celebrity and leaves the island for the first time to seek his fortune in Glasgow. His performances at the 'Café Bingo' attract attention. His fame spreads — and goes to his head!

A neglected and disgruntled Mairileen follows him to Glasgow and, angered by his lukewarm reception, breaks the chanter over his head. This also breaks the spell and Angus, unable to enchant his audiences with the chanter, decides to give them a song instead. Rejected by his former fans we come to the end of the first, but not the last, adventure of Angus Og.

'He's a Highland Beatnik,' says artist Ewen Bain.

This was the heading which introduced Angus Og to readers of the Glasgow *Bulletin* in 1960. 'Beatnik' was the popular expression of the time for young people who hoped to shock their elders by dress or behaviour intended to be outrageous or unconventional. Angus Og has succeeded in achieving this aim in various exploits throughout the years.

Though by now 'in real terms' he should be approaching 50 years of age, he remains eternally young and incorrigible. In this, the first story, he says to himself, 'I wonder where Auld Nick and the dancing girls is?'

In the last, unfinished story in December 1989 he is again about to tangle with Auld Nick. This time, sadly, we will never know how the encounter would have ended.

Angus may have remained eternally young in spirit but it is interesting to observe how his appearance has changed as Ewen's style developed over 30 years. Perhaps tribute should be paid to the editor of the *Bulletin* who recognised the potential in these early drawings.

Angus's early adoration for the sonsy Mairileen changed from the first frame in the *Bulletin* — 'Ochone it's myself that's lonely since Mairileen went off to work in the distillery.' By the time we reach the end of the story, Angus is proving to be happily unfaithful as, with the help of the enchanted chanter, he becomes the idol of the Café Bingo. Mairileen deserves an award for stamina for pursuing Angus so faithfully through all the adventures. 'Mairileen', incidentally, is Ewen's Utter Hebridean version of Marilyn which was a popular name for girls when Marilyn Monroe was at the height of her fame.

Ewen's allegiance to both Glasgow and the Highlands is clearly shown from the beginning of Angus Og. Though Angus lives on Drambeg he occasionally leaves the island to seek his fortune. It is appropriate that his first sortie should be to Glasgow thanks to 'the wee man' who made the chanter so enchanting.

Ewen and I both liked 'the wee man' but when Angus Og moved to the *Daily Record* the editor advised Ewen to base his ideas more on reality than on magic. Ewen took this advice; 'the wee man' vanished; but there are always magical moments in the world around us and Ewen was a wizard at finding and exploiting them.

The music which Ewen produced on his own chanter could not in fairness be described as enchanting but he could play a recognisable version of 'The Dark Island', having played the bagpipes in the Boys' Brigade band. Another accomplishment was the mouth organ and recently I found in his desk drawer a surprise which I had bought for him — a chromatic harmonica, the Larry Adler Professional 12.

Ewen, unlike his creation, Angus Og, never became big-headed with success. Perhaps he had noticed that with some celebrities 'pride goeth before a fall' because when Angus developed a 'guid conceit o' himself' he always came a cropper. Angus, like Ewen, was an optimist and, undeterred by the occasional disappointment, soon bounced back on his feet again ready for his next adventure. After Mairileen has scuppered his plans he has a few philosophical and indeed prophetical thoughts: 'I'm a broken man — I'll maybe throw myself in the Clyde — but that would be no use, I can't swim. Ah well! I've got my youth and my looks — something is sure to turn up!'

AND ANGUS STRIDES CONFIDENTLY INTO THE FUTURE.

ANGUS RACES HOME TO TELL HIS MOTHER OF HIS ENCOUNTER WITH 9 ONE OF THE 'WEE FOLK'.

ANGUS PLAYS THE ENCHANTED CHANTER FOR HIS MOTHER.

10

AS NIGHT FALLS OVER THE LONELY HEBRIDES THE ISLANDERS LISTEN ENTRANCED.

Ah well, it had to come some day ~ it's not so warm as I thought it would be.

I wonder where Auld Nick and the dancing girls is?

I'll go and see if there is anyone I know here.

My goodness ~ what is that terrible noise?

~ it is "himself" and he's after me!

HELP!

HE SEES AN OPENING IN THE WALL AND DIVES IN ~

1965

ANGUS OG AND THE PEAT REEK

A 'towrist' who asks if he can buy one of the Og peats as a souvenir gives Angus an idea for a money-making venture.

This becomes an international success with expatriates and eventually Mairileen (to get her out of the way) is sent abroad as an 'outside representative'. However, her expenses are lavish and she is recalled.

Angus falls foul of Granny McBrochan and the peat-reek enterprise goes up with a bang!

It could only be a 'towrist' who would want to take a peat home as a souvenir — or would it?

Ewen, the man who never wanted to be taken for a 'towrist' when on holiday in other parts of the Highlands, was happy to stow a few peats in the boot of the car when returning from visits to Skye.

Conditions had to be favourable for the peat-reek ritual to begin. It was at its most evocative on a dry, crisp evening in winter with a black sky sparkling with stars. A gentle breath of air would not go amiss for wafting the peat reek from the chimney to the appreciative sniffers below. On such an evening, without announcing his intention, Ewen would appear with a peat stored from the summer and with satisfaction place it on the fire. When it was glowing red we would stand shivering outside to savour to the full the distinctive aroma in the cold night air.

Not content with this, he would complete the ritual by coming indoors to engage in the potentially hazardous practice of placing on a small, metal shovel a portion of the still-glowing peat and wafting the smoke round the room. With nostalgia I could then, as now, easily picture us standing at the crossroads looking down the hill towards Staffin Bay with soft, grey peat-smoke curling from the chimneys of the houses below.

Nostalgic it might be but, as you might expect with Ewen, the ritual could not be taken too seriously and we always enjoyed the fun.

Angus Og, of course, having a keener interest in business than his creator, was quickly launched on another idea — for making money out of shredded peat. Angus anticipated Enterprise Scotland by several years, only he, being a bit of a genial twister, could not for morality, the example to our youth and the humour in his inevitable disasters, appear to prosper for too long.

Some of the ideas that Ewen devised for Angus's enterprises, however, seemed to me to have commercial possibilities for someone with marketing flair. As Ewen's time was fully occupied in drawing cartoons he would never have been bothered with the 'hassle' involved in launching and developing such ventures. He was much happier dreaming them up on paper for Angus to exploit.

Ewen was ever ready, as far as deadlines allowed, to comment on topicalities, and politicians provided much inspiration. It is interesting to return to the Sixties when Harold Wilson, with pipe, George Brown and President Lyndon B. Johnson were hitting the headlines.

Ewen leaves the Ogs without the comfort of the peat fire, huddled round an old paraffin-heater which looks suspiciously like the one which the previous owners of our house left behind.

1983

THE LISTENERS

Donald brings home a magical ear-trumpet which enables Angus to listen in to conversations some distance away. He overhears the Laird planning to sell Drambeg to an Arab Sheikh who later intends to ship the island, piece by piece, to the Persian Gulf.

Mairileen starts a keep-fit class for the overweight ladies of Drambeg.

The magical ear-trumpet falls into the hands of the DHSS with dire results for some of their clients.

The Sheikh imposes Muslim Law — for example, no drinking! — and takes a fancy to Mairileen.

The Rev. McSonachan finds the ear-trumpet and does not like what he hears. Sadly for Angus, Lachie flattens the ear-trumpet.

Mairileen leads a female revolt against Islam/Presbyterian rule and imposes female rule with compulsory marriage for men. This sickens the Sheikh and he returns to the Gulf.

'Neffer mind your toes then, Effie — see if you can touch your knees!'

This could have been overheard at Miss McRory's slimming class as Mairileen offered a word of encouragement to Effie the postmistress. Ewen had no need to attend slimming classes. He took a batch of cartoons into the *Daily Record* wearing a brown leather jacket and someone told him that he looked like a wallet.

'I never liked it anyway!' he said as I looked aghast at his attempt to press the lapels with a damp cloth. Perhaps it was destined for the jumble sale and someone who liked a bargain with wrinkled lapels — Donald Og perhaps?

Serendipity, the art of making happy chance finds, was more to Ewen's liking in the open air than at a jumble sale in a church hall. From a small, disused quarry filled with loads of builders' rubble he and the dog unearthed and brought home their muddy treasures. I didn't get the magic ear-trumpet which I could do with now but who would like a ribbed-glass scrubbing board?

Ewen would have loved that ear-trumpet, though he managed very well with his own ears! He was certainly visually observant. He was also a good listener. All I will state is that people should be very careful about what they say in restaurants — you never know who is listening! I regularly found that I was talking to myself as Ewen, entranced, overheard some gem from a neighbouring table.

How the plot developed — with Mairileen and her 'monstrous regiment of women'; compulsory marriage for men; and the Sheikh proposing to ship Drambeg to the Persian Gulf — was a mystery shared by Ewen. Invariably, when he started a new story he had not the faintest idea of how it would finish.

Earlier in his career he was asked to provide scripts for each story. He reluctantly complied with the request but I doubt if even one plot followed the original submission. Gradually he was left to develop the situations in his own style with the flexibility and spontaneity to make use of items of topical interest.

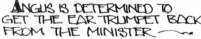

C880

C881

C886

C887

SLAINTE, LACHIE - IT'S GOOD BEING ABLE TO HAVE A LEGITIMATE DRAM AGAIN!

SO IT IS, ANGUS - AND WE OWE IT ALL TO OUR PRESIDENT, MAIRILEEN!

BAR

I HEAR SHE'S APPOINTING A VICE-PRESIDENT.

THAT'S CHUST WHAT THIS ISLAND HAS BEEN NEEDING - I WONDER WHO IT WILL BE?

PROBABLY GRANNY McBROCHAN!

WHY NOT BIG MAGGIE McMAY- SHE'S GOT A LOT OF EXPERIENCE

C888

?

THERE ARE GOING TO BE SOME CHANGES ON DRAMBEG, LADIES, NOW THAT WE'RE IN CHARGE OF THINGS!

HOORAY!

NOT BEFORE TIME!

WHEN YOU'VE FINISHED THOSE DISHES GO AND BRING IN SOME PEATS!

AND SEE THEY'RE ALL IN THEIR BED BY THE TIME I COME BACK FROM THE CEILIDH!

WE'RE STARVING - WHAT ARE YOU MAKING FOR OUR TEA?

C889

I SAY, LOOK AT THIS — SHEIK ALI BEN OOVI WANTS TO SELL DRAMBEG — BUT HE CAN'T FIND A BUYER!

UTTER HEBRIDEAN GAZETTE OVERSEAS EDITION.

GOOD LUCK TO HIM!

BUT IT WAS YOUR FAMILY SEAT, FINGAL DEAR — WOULDN'T YOU LIKE TO GO BACK THERE?

GAD NO — IT'S MUCH MORE PLEASANT HERE IN THE WEST INDIES —

BASKING IN THE SUN IN THIS ISLAND PARADISE WITH THE BRITISH NAVY ON HAND TO KEEP THE PEACE —

WHY ARE THEY FLYING THE STARS AND STRIPES?

HELLO — I'D LIKE TO MAKE A CALL TO SHEIK ALI BEN OOVI!

YOUR MOTHER IS STILL LAID UP THEN, ANGUS.

YES SHE IS, LACHIE — HOW DID YOU KNOW?

IT'LL BE A WEE WHILE BEFORE HERSELF AND THE OTHER KEEP-FIT ADDICTS ARE FIT AGAIN.

HERE, ANGUS — I'VE CHUST HEARD THAT THE SHEIK IS AWAY — AND HE'S SOLD THE ISLAND BACK TO OUR OLD LAIRD, FINGAL DRAMBEG OF DRAMBEG!

C897

THANK GOODNESS — FOR FINGAL IS OUR FELLOW-COUNTRYMAN — A MAN WHO VERY NEARLY SPEAKS THE SAME LANGUAGE AS OURSELVES!

GAD MABEL, OLD GAL — IT'S FRIGHTFULLY NAICE BEING BACK HEAH IN JOLLY OLD DRAMBEG, WHAT!

1984

INSTANT THRIFT

Mrs Og, using a jam jar as a vase, arranges a bunch of thrift which she has gathered near the shore. The water in which the flowers were placed has a curious effect on her — she becomes most concerned about spendthrift ways.

Wily Angus put the 'Water of Thrift' on the market as a cure for extravagance. This proves to be successful in many different situations until the effect wears off and extravagance returns — enhanced!

An outbreak of prodigality sweeps Drambeg before the crisis is reached and resolved and the island returns to normal.

'An old jam jar will save me using a vase,' said Mrs Og. Ewen might have said, 'Two old jam jars will save me buying designer water-pots.' One stained black from washing Indian ink from his brushes and old-fashioned nibs and another stained white from poster paint still sit on his desk. It was simply that he continued to use the jars from force of habit, like the white, wooden chair which was beginning to fall apart from age and now sits forlorn, held together with black, sticky tape.

Lest I should give the wrong impression, Ewen was the most generous of husbands though he never quite came to terms with decimalisation and would still refer to ten pence coins as florins. As long as he was earning enough for our needs he was not interested in family finances — someone had to do it and he was quite happy to leave that responsibility to me. When three of us were living on his teacher's salary — £36 monthly — he came home on pay day and, laughing, threw the notes in the air just like several of the characters in the 'Instant Thrift' story. He may have been clowning but our drop in income when I stopped teaching was the motivation he needed to start drawing the cartoons.

Whenever we were involved in a difficult situation we would agree that we would see the funny side of it — some day! — or, that it would provide grist for the mill. Sometimes it did and I would recognise the source of inspiration when I saw it in one of the cartoons. This could be anything from Ewen's dislike of finding bones in fish to the disinclination of some 'foreigners' to accept Scottish banknotes. The seagull's 'splatt' on the head of the official from the Department of Frugality was inspired by the one which landed on Ewen's head. Going to bed at ten p.m. to save burning lights was a reminder of the hotel owner who practised this economy on his guests without warning and left us stumbling upstairs in the dark.

'It's the thrift water — I'm thinking of putting it on the market!' said Angus to Lachie. Ewen never had any inclination to market anything, even when he was given a wine-making kit by our daughter.

'Would you like a glass of my home-made wine?' he said to me one day. Not particularly, I thought, having sampled it already, but said bravely, 'Yes, that would be lovely!'

At that time I had a swelling behind a tooth with a suspected abscess. After one glass of Ewen's extremely dry wine I was aware to my delight that the swelling had disappeared. When I told our dentist about this he said, 'Get some of it and we'll put it on the market!'

If Angus Og instead of Ewen had heard of that suggestion, he would have been on his way to making another fortune.

1986

THE BY-ELECTION

Following a bump on the head Angus becomes good and honest.

Impressing the electorate, he gains a majority as an Independent candidate in the District Council By-Election.

After a second bump on the head caused by Mairileen's ardour he returns to normal.

Mairileen obtains a passion potion from Granny McBrochan with unexpected results, one of which is a plague of giant midges with predictable effects, the most important being that the investigation of a suitable site on Drambeg for nuclear dumping is abandoned.

'Did you know that our Angus had fallen off the ladder yesterday and landed on his head?' said Donald to Mrs Og.

'I wondered what had caused the improvement,' she replied.

Many mothers, exasperated with their offsprings' untidiness, would have been as astonished as Mrs Og to hear that they had been overcome by an urge to clean the house — though falling on their heads might be considered a rather drastic remedy. Even if the transformation did not last, it would make a pleasant change from constant nagging or shutting the door on the accumulated mess, which seem to be the two most popular ways of dealing with the problem.

The transformation did last long enough for Angus, still suffering from his 'attack of goodness', to be selected as an Independent candidate for the District Council By-Election. Some prospective candidates could take a few tips on winning votes according to Angus's disgruntled opposition — 'That blighter Og is stooping to some very low tactics in this campaign!'

Ewen won quite a few votes from me from his 'attack of goodness' on household chores, though they could not be predicted. 'I don't like being asked to do things,' he would say. This made household management somewhat difficult in our reversal of roles for Angus had nothing on Ewen when it came to powers of persuasion.

When Ewen decided that the time had come to make cartooning a full-time occupation he suggested that I should return to teaching. 'It would rejuvenate you,' he said. I didn't quite know how to take this remark and, of course, it could not have been the extra money or having the house to himself during the day which prompted it. Nevertheless, a short time later I was driving each morning into rush-hour traffic and facing the challenge of the classroom from which a grateful Ewen had escaped to walk the dog in sunlit fields.

He always admitted that there was a lot of himself in Angus!

We heard later, to our wry amusement, that an acquaintance had said, 'Fancy giving up his job and sending his wife out to work while he stays at home doing nothing all day.' Another said to him quite seriously, 'Tell me, do you really call that work?'

Ewen did exercise the dog, in all weathers, but he left the sunshine outside and returned to his desk. It was work — and hard work at that! The Rev. McSonachan expressed the feeling with which Ewen was so familiar: 'Dear me — Saturday afternoon and I still haven't thought of an idea for tomorrow's sermon! Whatever am I to do?'

Ewen knew what he had to do — work long after midnight if necessary and be at his desk early next morning to meet the deadlines. By some miracle he always did!

Perhaps, like the Rev. McSonachan, he could have asked Angus to help him. Come to think of it, perhaps he did: when asked to appear on a religious programme for children's television he was heard to say, '. . . and this is little Noah in the bulrushes.'

Considering his upbringing, listening regularly to sermons in Gaelic, this was obviously a slip of the tongue. Despite his fondness for using biblical texts in appropriate situations, he was not a churchgoer in adult life, describing himself as 'a lapsed Free Presbyterian'.

Perhaps to balance the biblical allusion a jovial 'Auld Nick' has appeared at intervals throughout the years, until his final attempt to trick Angus in Ewen's last, unfinished story.

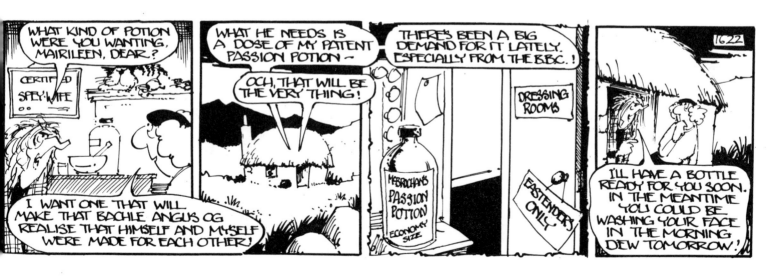

I THINK MY PLAN WITH THE POTION FOR ANGUS HAS GONE WRONG!

DIST. COUNCIL OFFICES

1627

QUICK, CONSTABLE - SOME OF THE CLEANSING COMMITTEE ARE TEARING OFF THEIR CLOTHES AND BEHAVING VERY ODDLY

I'M NOT SURPRISED - HAVE YOU TRIED TURNING THE CENTRAL HEATING DOWN?

GOODNESS ME. WE DON'T HAVE THE COUNCIL HEATING -

TURNED UP AS HIGH AS ALL THAT -

IN THESE TIMES OF STRINGENT ECONOMIES!

DID YOU BRING UP OUR TRIP TO MEXICO AT YOUR MEETING LAST NIGHT, ANGUS?

I COULDN'T, LACHIE - SOME OF THE CLEANSING COMMITTEE HAD GOT OVER-EXCITED FOR SOME REASON!

1628

PERHAPS IF I WAS TO ADD IT TO A HALF BOTTLE OF HIS FAVOURITE TIPPLE?

HALF OF THIS PASSION POTION HAS BEEN WASTED - I'LL HAVE TO MAKE SURE THAT ANGUS GETS THE REST OF IT!

DRAMBEG STORES.

DO YOU HAVE A HALF BOTTLE OF FINE OLD DRAMBEG DEW · OR BEN OOM MALT · OR McALLISTER'S DELIGHT · OR CREAM O' THE MOOR OR OLD BRACKEN SPECIAL · OR ANY OTHER BLEND · OR SINGLE OR DOUBLE MALT AT ALL AT ALL?

SPECIAL OFFER

WHAT ABOUT A NICE TEN YEAR OLD FUJIYAMA?

1986–7

THE GREAT GOSUGNA

Angus discovers that he has hypnotic powers and, after testing them on various subjects, decides to tread the boards as 'The Great Gosugna' (Angus Og spelled backwards). He is a great success and puts a van on the road for private consultations.

A case of mistaken identity with a Russian traitor who defected with state secrets brings two Russian agents to Drambeg.

Angus is then employed by the District Council as their official hypnotist: 'To hypnotise any ratepayers who might be having little problems.'

Mairileen finds that Angus has been deceiving her and thumps him on the eye. His hypnotic powers end, and Angus falls foul of more than Mairileen.

Another enterprising bubble bursts, and Angus and Drambeg return to normal.

It was the sea safari to the only drive-in volcano in the world — Soufrière in St Lucia — that provided the inspiration for the Great Gosugna. The passengers were in convivial mood on the brig — a two-masted, square-rigged vessel — on which we sailed the Spanish Main. The sun was shining and the rum punch was liberally flowing into plastic tumblers, albeit with a warning about the man who had imbibed too freely on a previous voyage. While being escorted through the crater of the volcano he had staggered and had accidentally plunged his foot into a pool of boiling, volcanic mud, with results best left to the imagination.

Mindful of this, Ewen was drinking no more than a 'small sensation' while enjoying a conversation with a cheerful man sitting next to him. He proved to be the hypnotist who was to entertain the passengers on the cruise ship later that evening. Mellowed by the sunshine, Ewen decided to watch the show but not to participate. Were it not for this chance encounter, the Great Gosugna might never have appeared in Drambeg.

We had never seen a hypnotist perform on stage, having had misgivings about the possible ill-effects on the poor victims who had been persuaded to participate. That evening we were astonished at the number of eager volunteers who needed no persuading whatsoever. When hypnotised, they were indeed very funny, but we still had doubts about its advisability.

This was Ewen's second visit to the Caribbean. At the end of the war the ship on which he served as a coder in the Royal Navy was sent on a goodwill tour of the West Indies. From the 'hazards' of convoy-escort duty between Gibraltar and West Africa, the most onerous task in the West Indies was having to make polite conversation with wealthy ladies who invited the sailors to their homes for afternoon tea.

It was not tea that an erring husband had been drinking while celebrating the festive season in Drambeg. His excuse, that being hypnotised by the Great Gosugna was responsible for his foolish appearance, met with a frosty reception from his irate wife.

'You're as hypnotised as a newt!' she shouted.

Work and the demon drink are uneasy companions and Ewen never touched it while he was working — which was most of the time! Inspiration does not keep office hours and we led what some would consider to be a very restricted social life. However, when relaxing, Ewen enjoyed a dram with friends and on these occasions he could be very entertaining. One anecdote followed another — often about various calamities which had befallen him through the years.

To see the funny side of life's difficulties is a wonderful gift and, of course, much of this is expressed in the cartoons, which also contained his comments on what he saw as social injustice.

THE GREAT GOSUGNA

1818

I'VE GOT SOMETHING IN MY EYE, ANGUS— CAN YOU SEE WHAT IT IS?

SIT IN THIS CHAIR AND I'LL HAVE A LOOK.

NO, I CAN'T SEE ANYTHING—

KEEP LOOKING ME STRAIGHT IN THE EYE—

TILL I HAVE A GOOD LOOK AND ——!

ZZZZ

HELP MY GOODNESS— SHE'S DROPPED OFF!

ARE YOU SAYING THAT YOUR MOTHER FELL ASLEEP WHEN YOU LOOKED IN HER EYE?

YES I AM, AND SHE WAS IN THE MIDDLE OF MAKING A CLOOTIE DUMPLING AT THE TIME!

WHERE'S YON SEMMIT I CHUST TOOK OFF?

ZZZZZ

1819

HOW LONG WAS SHE ASLEEP?

I DON'T KNOW YET— THAT'S WHY I HAD TO BUY THIS BOOK— AH YES, HERE WE ARE —

TEACH YOURSELF HYPNOTISM

I'LL BE BACK IN A MINUTE—!

SNAP!

GOODNESS— I MUST HAVE DOZED OFF!

Panel 1: HELLO, HERE'S COUNCILLOR HAGGISBOTTOM COMING — AWAY AND OPEN THE DOOR FOR HIM, ANGUS!

Panel 2: YOU'RE THE VERY MAN I WANT TO SEE — I WANTED TO THANK YOU FOR HELPING MY OLD AUNT, MRS McCHITTER! / OCH IT WAS NOTHING!

Panel 3: SHE TELLS ME YOU CHUST HAD A FEW WORDS WITH HER AND SHE HASN'T FELT THE COLD SINCE! / I GAVE HER A WEE TOUCH OF HYPNOTISM — FOR HER WHOLE HOUSE WAS FREEZING! / 1858

Panel 4: IT STILL IS — BUT NOW SHE DOESN'T FEEL IT! / THE DISTRICT COUNCIL HAS DECIDED TO TAKE ON A HYPNOTIST — WOULD YOU LIKE THE JOB? / OCH I'D HAVE TO THINK ABOUT IT — YES, I'LL TAKE IT!

Panel 5: I'VE BEEN OFFERED A JOB, MOTHER / WHAT KIND OF JOB? / AS DISTRICT COUNCIL HYPNOTIST! / 1859

Panel 6: BUT I THOUGHT THEY WERE ALREADY IN A TRANCE! / NO, NO — IT'S NOT TO HYPNOTISE THE COUNCILLORS —

Panel 7: IT'S TO HYPNOTISE ANY RATEPAYERS WHO MIGHT BE HAVING LITTLE PROBLEMS!

Panel 8: — AND WHEN I SNAP MY FINGERS YOU'LL WAKE UP AND FIND YOURSELF HAVING A PADDLE IN BENIDORM — AND IT'S NOT A BURST PIPE AT ALL! / ZZZZ